Parental Mental Health

FACTORING IN FATHERS

Parental Mental Health

FACTORING IN FATHERS

Jane I. Honikman & Daniel B. Singley

Contents

ABOUT THIS BOOK

We have written this book because men have not been well-represented in the parental mental health movement. While we have advanced our understanding of maternal mental health, the field, as a whole, has failed to include their partners. We are feminists and see men and women as equals, while acknowledging key differences. We want to shift the focus of the maternal mental health movement to a *parental* mental health approach that includes the mental well-being of all parents, no matter what the gender. This includes mental wellness beyond the perinatal period.

The purpose of this book is to include men in the discussion about early parenthood, to foster a gender-equitable, whole-family approach to parental mental health, and to increase awareness about best practices in the care for expectant and new fathers. For example, although people commonly use the term "postpartum" to mean "postpartum depression" in mothers, the research clearly shows that dads often experience a range of mental health concerns at rates that are comparable to those of mothers:

- 4–16% anxiety in expectant fathers
- 2.4–18% anxiety in postpartum fathers
- 10% postpartum depression in fathers

Our approach uses a feminist intersectional lens that addresses a variety of dimensions of diversity, including ethnicity, gender, sexual orientation, and socio-economic status. This book describes the common barriers that fathers and health care providers alike experience in factoring in the fathers.

OPEN LETTERS FROM JANE AND DAN

Jane Honikman's Feminist Lens

I was raised in the traditional decade of the 1950s and impacted by the social change years of the 1960s and 1970s. It was an exciting time to be a young woman in the 1960s. We rebelled against being told our hemlines had to cover our knees. It was offensive to play basketball on a half court with a three-dribble limit. Those are trivial personal examples of inequality but reflective of the wider social and political upheavals surrounding me. I watched the marches on Washington against the war in Vietnam and the brutality against civil rights activists. These fueled my thoughts about equity and equality in American society.

My childhood "career" goal was to become a wife and mother. My favorite book in high school had been "Dear Abby's Letters of Advice." The primary message was how to remain a virgin until marriage and obey one's husband. Women's sexuality was a forbidden topic. Birth control options were not discussed. That changed with the revolutionary book, *Our Bodies, Ourselves,* published in the 1960s. I was swept into the women's movement's promotion of equality, equity, and empowerment. The emphasis was on education and consciousness raising. What had been taboo topics became public. First, it was birth control. Next, it was our breasts, uterus, ovaries, conception, pregnancy, labor and birth, and breastfeeding. We spoke about reproductive hormones and their cycles. There was a sense of both relief and dismay. Could we be in control of our emotions and moods? Is it mind over matter, or is it the brain? We questioned, argued, and debated the changing traditional roles of men and women.

In 1965, I was pregnant, single, and alone. I was in denial. I gave birth in a foreign country and never saw my baby. She was adopted. I felt shame, guilt, and embarrassment. I had no emotional support.

Several years later, I married the father of our first born and we got pregnant again. I gave birth with a supportive husband but away from extended family and with few friends. We had no emotional support. My experiences motivated me to become a feminist activist.

It was a time of massive social change and action. Men and women worked together on confronting discrimination, poverty, injustice, racism, ageism, sexism, and war. Expectations and stereotypes were challenged. This included becoming parents. It was not just a woman's issue!

The childbirth education movement began while we were pregnant in the 1970s. Women were determined to take charge of their pregnancies, labors, and deliveries. My husband was given the opportunity to attend birth classes. We wanted a family, and we were going to greet our newborn together. The classes taught breathing techniques for labor and delivery, but no one prepared us for the reality of becoming parents. It was a shock!

Our friends agreed with this lopsided emphasis on birth and not parenthood. We would meet with our babies and share the realities versus our expectations; the highs and lows of being parents. Although the husbands were acknowledged, it was the mothers who were gathering. It felt good.

We wondered if there might be a way to expand our social support gatherings into a community-wide network. Four of us decided to try, and we founded Postpartum Education for Parents (PEP). On July 1, 1977, we launched a 24/7 telephone support line called a "Warmline" followed by new parent support groups (www.sbpep.org) run entirely by volunteers. Based on our own experiences, we created a "chart of common feelings" for mothers and fathers.

Shared Parental Emotions	No Gender Differences
Overwhelmed	Resentment/Jealousy
Sexual Frustration	Inadequate
Insecure	Trapped/Lonely
Depressed/Weepy	Loving/Thankful
Panic	Irritation
Excited/Satisfaction	Tired

The founders of PEP wrote this list of commonly expressed emotional reactions to new parenthood. We had no knowledge of mental illness. These were our own unexpected, conflicting, and sometimes "forbidden" emotions. PEP and these words were published in a 1983 book called *The Private Life of Parents.* They formed the basis of PEP volunteer training.

As the name states, PEP is for parents, not just mothers. The founders believed that everyone needs and deserves emotional support after the arrival of a newborn. Our focus was on community-based, peer-to-peer social support. We became trained parent volunteers. What we created was unique, and we received national media attention.

I became the spokesperson for PEP. I responded to calls from people wanting to start a PEP in their own community, and from researchers and journalists looking for a story. In 1983, a woman was researching for her book about postpartum depression. She asked me how many calls about depression we had received on the "Warmline."

I replied, "I don't know. I'm not sure what you're asking."

That conversation changed my life and connected me to the world of psychiatry and psychology. I knew nothing about mental illness and was overwhelmed to discover a century of scientific research on motherhood and madness. It was the polar opposite of PEP's non-medical approach to ease the adjustment to parenthood through social support. I needed to learn more.

I began to meet the world leaders of the postpartum scientific movement. Their focus was on mental illness. The woman's body changes through conceiving, growing, and birthing a new life. It made sense that the scientists were looking for explanations why one in ten mothers experienced major depression and one in a thousand suffered a psychosis. The research studies ranged from causes, medical treatments, and clinical interventions. I listened to reports at conferences and read research papers trying to decipher this information. It was fascinating and terrifying. Was it the hormones? What about heredity? I learned about medications, psychotherapy, and mother and baby units in psychiatric hospitals. No one mentioned new fathers.

After being exposed to this affront to the myth of parenthood, I felt it was time to galvanize the suffering women and their families into a social movement. I had connected with support organizations that worked specifically with postpartum depression. Yet I struggled calling this a "women's issue." How did this extreme reaction to childbirth have a place in the world of parenthood? How did the men fit into this picture?

Women were entering the workforce. There was an enormous need for quality childcare and few options. I became involved with the National Family Resource movement, an advocate for parent support, and learning how to navigate and balance work and family.

I founded Postpartum Support International in 1987. My vision for PSI has always been the development of parent support networks in every community in the world with an emphasis on inclusion, emotional support, prevention, and wellness. The basis of my point of view comes from being a feminist. Social norms change through advocacy and activism. It is paramount to have heartfelt conversations about how fathers are viewed today. As we celebrate the role of fathers in all cultures, we recognize and acknowledge the power and importance of parental mental health.

In the 1990s, researchers began to study the brain's own hormones and chemical transmitters. It is not only about the woman's reproductive system. Heredity, sleep deprivation, trauma, and stress over lifestyle changes are not limited to biological mothers. This may explain why fathers and adoptive parents can also suffer from postpartum depression.

There has been astonishing medical progress about brain diseases and mental illness in this twenty-first century. Governments, businesses, and not-for-profit organizations throughout the world have invested financial and social capital to increase awareness. Campaigns are featured on television, at bus stops, and on social media. The maternal mental health movement encourages screening during pregnancy and following the birth. The question remains, what about the father?

Daniel Singley's Journey from Dude to Dad Researcher

Fifteen years ago, when my wife was pregnant with our older son, I had a series of interactions with close friends and even some family members that went something like this:

[Friend says to my wife]: "You're going to be the best mom, you're absolutely glowing. You're going to flower as a woman. You're so lucky!"

[The same friend turns to me]: "You're screwed. You'll never surf again, and you better get used to being broke and having zero work-life balance."

Those interactions were equally scary and frustrating for me, and thankfully my experience as a father has been a fantastic journey, which I've treasured. Like a lot of dads these days, I was dead set on being super involved throughout the pregnancy, birth, and the immediate postpartum "fourth trimester." I was unaware, however, of any resources for new or expectant dads. I found myself caught in what I've come to think of as the "fatherhood generation gap," in which fathers are expected to be highly engaged throughout the perinatal period, spanning from conception to a year or two postpartum, even though we don't really have models or a playbook for how to go about it because stereotypically, our own fathers weren't particularly involved during this period.

The work of Jane and her colleagues, along with many other feminist and women's liberation pioneers in the '60s and '70s, set the stage for women to have increasingly more options and visibility taking part in traditionally masculine areas, especially work. As women have become more involved in professional endeavors, the domestic duties involved in having a family haven't gone anywhere. While many women are faced with the daunting "second shift" of handling all the family logistics on top of working an eight-hour day (or longer), so are fathers naturally becoming more involved in cooking, cleaning, and caring for even very young children and babies. In fact, as men's gender roles shift, nowhere is this change more visible than the increased focus on the need for fathers to be highly engaged with their children and partners. Although gender roles in the U.S. are gradually trending toward equality, as a society, we haven't really carved out spaces for men to be seen as particularly valued by society for inhabiting traditionally female spaces (e.g. stay-at-home dads, healing professions such as nurses, doulas, midwives), which parallels the increasing understanding of the importance of including women in the professional arena.

It's important to recognize that throughout five years of doctoral study in psychology—including a course on gender—at no point did anyone discuss the psychology of men, men's issues, or masculinity. It wasn't until I came out to do my clinical internship at the University of California, San Diego's Counseling Center that a local psychologist specializing in men's issues and fatherhood came to talk to my internship class. He blew my mind by talking about the psychosocial changes of new fatherhood, masked male depression, normative male alexithymia, and a host of other now-familiar concepts that I had never heard of. I didn't even realize that men's issues was a "thing" in psychology! I immediately began getting familiar with research and practice about masculinity and because I had an infant at the time, I focused heavily on early fatherhood. This focus clarified for me that there was a real lack of emphasis on the role of fathers in the area of "maternal mental health" and the more I learned, the better able I was to see a clear need for mental health professionals to include fathers in their perspectives of early parenthood. Along the way, I found Postpartum Support International, which has become very much my family and a professional home. While of course there is more work to be done in factoring in fathers and taking a more gender-inclusive frame, I've been thrilled to find bright, likeminded folks in the organization that Jane founded who are also looking to push the pendulum forward to include dads in the parental mental health conversation.

The program of research I have been leading for the past 13 years focuses on deepening our understanding of fathers' involvement with their infants. Over the years, my team and I have worked hard to develop a more nuanced, multidimensional understanding of what fathers' involvement with their infants and babies looks like in today's world. Along the way, our work has involved the development of the Paternal Involvement with Infants Scale (Singley, et al., 2018) in which dads get to report their own involvement instead of researchers relying on their partners' impressions. We have also put the father at the heart of our methodologies by looking at how different factors such as relationship satisfaction, the parental alliance, gender role conflict, social support, depression, and anxiety relate to how dads are involved with their babies. Most previous research in this area looked at how dads' involvement impacted the baby and his partner—but our focus looks at the father's involvement with his baby and his partner in terms of how it impacts him. As this program of research continues, we have just validated the PIWIS survey for use with Latino dads and we're also using a strengths-based positive psychological lens as we factor in the fathers.

As a researcher and a therapist, I have dedicated my life to working with men and fathers to help them and their loved ones to experience richer, more fulfilling lives. Often, research on paternal engagement has focused exclusively on how dads' involvement impacts their children and partners. As part of our effort to address contemporary parental mental health more broadly, we aim to shed light on the critical needs and issues that fathers and father figures experience, in order to empower them to be as involved as possible with their families. I frequently encounter what I call the "zero sum game" approach, which suggests that by emphasizing fathers, we somehow detract from or marginalize mothers. On the contrary, volumes of research have shown that by focusing on helping dads to be the best, most involved fathers and partners they can be, the whole family is healthier. In that sense, focusing on fathers' needs and mental health is very much a women's issue but more broadly, it's just the other half of the parental mental health issue. The different lifestyle changes that new parents experience aren't limited just to biological mothers. Finally, although we will be using heteronormative language throughout this book that may sound like we're talking just about traditional male-female couples, we want to be clear that this information is relevant to dads, partners, father figures, nongestational parents, and parents of all genders. This book is ABOUT dads, and it's FOR everyone!

Chapter 1

THE FACTS

The fact is, an egg requires a sperm for pregnancy. The woman's body and the developing fetus become the focus of attention. What about the "pregnant" man? Who listens to his joys and fears? In this chapter, we look at masculinity and how a dad's gender plays into the overall experience as a parent, partner, or friend.

To take a close look at dads, we ask what it means to be a man. Masculinity is the foundation on which we build the fatherhood role. These days, hearing the term, "masculinity" often conjures up the concept of "toxic masculinity" which basically refers to a male who lives by a rigid, old-school version of masculinity which can be harmful to others and to himself. Masculinities are like any other personality trait or strength—if used in an overly-rigid way without consideration of how to be flexible and adaptive, they become problematic. "Masculinity" refers to gender and means how a person identifies in terms of being male. Gender is often related to, but is different from, a person's sexual/affection orientation, which is about what gender you're attracted to.

Traditional Masculinity: Dad 1.0

Early research is founded on a large cross-cultural study done in the mid-1970s that asked males what they thought it meant to be a man. (David & Brannon, 1976). A four-sided "man box" emerged.

1. Anti-femininity: "No Sissy Stuff"
2. Status and Achievement: "The Big Wheel"
3. Inexpressiveness and Independence: "The Sturdy Oak"
4. Adventurousness and Aggressiveness: "Give 'Em Hell"

Anti-femininity was found to be the strongest, most consistent aspect of masculinity across cultures. It means that whatever it entails to be a woman or feminine in your culture, being a "traditional" man simply means not being feminine. The traditional "guy-guy" role is reactive and the strongest indicator of whether you're being manly; you are NOT being feminine. For new and expectant fathers, this has important implications because most societies frame pregnancy, birth, and the raising of infants as being "women's work." Fathers taking part in this aspect of their lives are stepping outside the "man box." The three other characteristics of traditional masculinity are:

- "The Big Wheel:" SUCCESSFUL Entertainers, politicians, military leaders, bosses and shot-callers.
- "The Sturdy Oak:" STRONG AND SILENT Types nothing knocks them off their spot and they don't need anyone.
- "Give 'Em Hell:" AGGRESSIVE RISK-TAKER Willing to fight, take risks, and be physically and sexually dominant.

In general, there is a spectrum of these traits. For the past thirty years, the psychological study of masculinity looked at what was wrong with men:

suicide, domestic violence, high mortality rates, drug use, and depression. The earliest research on fathers tended to focus on being absent or abusive and causing problems for their families. More recently, a new group of researchers has begun to focus on what's RIGHT with men, the Positive Psychology/Positive Masculinities approach (Kiselica & Englar-Carlson, 2010). This complements the traditional negatively-focused masculinity research.

In Dan's practice in Southern California, many of the dads he sees are more "out of the box" guys who see themselves as a good teammate who:

- Compromises with his partner
- Shows emotional openness
- Expresses empathy
- Is available

However, as we will see, in order for these dads to show the traits that help them to be the best fathers and partners they can be, they have to push past some of the problematic norms that society teaches them about what it means to be a "real man."

Gender Role Strain and Precarious Manhood

The concept of gender role strain refers to the feeling of stress that a person experiences when he acts differently from what is expected by his society's usual norms for men. If he doesn't match up to the typical "guy-guy" social norm, he runs the risk of experiencing a psychological strain (Pleck, 1981). This can result in stress, irritability, and physical aggression. This may mean shutting down and checking out of the hands-on duties of caring for an infant. Social norms are changing so that men are expected to be more involved with their babies' and partners' lives than ever before. The issue is that while this shift toward more involvement is happening, the current generation of dads most likely didn't have role models because their own fathers were probably not very involved during pregnancy, birth, and the first year postpartum. This newer expectation has dads carrying their babies, giving bottles, changing diapers, and being involved with their babies' eating and sleeping schedule. This scenario often creates a conflict with the antifemininity pillar of traditional Dad 1.0, and can result in him experiencing the stress of gender role strain which may make him less likely to do these behaviors.

Another key theme is the idea of "precarious manhood" (Vandello & Bosson, 2013). This means that a man's sense of being manly is both difficult to establish and dangerously easy to threaten. This research suggests that the traditional feminine or womanly identity comes from her natural and biological processes of menstruation, pregnancy, lactation, and menopause. Traditional "guyness," on the other hand, has to be earned and maintained over and over again in ways that prove to others and himself that he's manly. Basically, you're only as manly as the last thing you did. You can lose your "man card" at any time if you're not careful. For new fathers who grew up with a more old-school model of dads as the stoic protector/provider who keeps the family fed and safe, the demands to be a loving co-parent who expresses stress or struggle with early fatherhood represent ongoing potential sources of shame or threats to his manliness.

An example about gender conflict in popular media is a 2018 tweet by Chris Evans, a.k.a. Marvel's Captain America. Piers Morgan, a British TV personality, tweeted a picture of Daniel "James Bond" Craig wearing his newborn and suggested the actor was being emasculated. Chris Evans's scathing tweet in response, and the thousands of comments that followed, shows the changing nature of new fatherhood and the expectation that taking care of kids, including babies, is in fact manly. And besides, how amazing is it to have Captain America standing up for James Bond's right to engage in baby-wearing?!

Biases and Barriers

One of the main points of this book is the need to include dads in the early parenthood journey. Beyond just "factoring in fathers," gender equality suggests the need to be more inclusive with more males as doulas (also known as "dude-las"), peer support facilitators, midwives, therapists, and lactation consultants. Forty years after the start of the women's liberation and feminist movement, society is in the middle of wrestling with the gender and social justice implications of the #metoo and "time's up" focus on empowering women and the wrongs that have been done by men. Framing men and dads as a marginalized group in need of support is provocative. The fact remains that men as health care providers and dads as health care consumers do experience barriers to being involved throughout the perinatal period.

Societal and Professional Biases

Written materials, social media, conferences, and conversations with clinicians or people looking to get help, generally use the term "maternal" instead of the broader and gender neutral "perinatal." We attend meetings when people refer to "maternal mental health" when in fact the topic being addressed isn't specific to moms or dads. It's about the role of parenting and the proximity to the birth, but "perinatal mental health" just isn't used as a term. This trend is changing. Having "maternal health" as the industry-standard term definitely turns people away from factoring in fathers as consumers. It also discourages some males from becoming more involved in the research, practice, and policy of perinatal mental health.

One key issue is how professionals in the field talk to—or even avoid—fathers about their role throughout the birth, pregnancy, and postpartum period. Dan's experience with friends and family was hearing that his life was over. This input mirrors what nurses, obstetricians, midwives, birth professionals, and even well-intentioned mental health practitioners commonly say to men. The short version of the advice is, "You be the rock and provide your partner with all the support she needs." That may be great advice, but like other stereotypes, it tends to take over and become the whole story. The bottom line is that the transition to parenthood is often a difficult adjustment no matter what the gender or background of the parent. No matter how great his partner is, no one person can meet all of his social support and connection needs—we're just not used to thinking of men as needing interpersonal connection outside of romance. Dads will absolutely need to get their own support from trusted friends, family, colleagues, clergy, and others. Unfortunately, professionals who have contact with fathers in the perinatal period rarely address the dad. The proactive dad will need to access social support outside of his relationship with his partner. Dan has spoken with fathers who felt out of place in hospitals, clinics, birthing centers, and well-baby visits because the professionals they interacted with didn't make eye contact or respond to their questions. They felt minimized in their role. It is a type of paternal "benign neglect."

The phenomenon of parental gatekeeping—which we will cover in more detail in Chapter 3—often reflects anxiety and avoidance. It also has a parallel at the level of professional development of males in the field of parental mental health and can discourage males from getting involved. Throughout Dan's career in psychology, he has been one of the few males in the room for supervision, research team meetings, and trainings. This experience has become even more common as he has focused on reproductive and perinatal mental health. He has experienced firsthand some of the beliefs and barriers that can discourage men from getting involved in perinatal mental health. Western society has feminized the phenomenon of a "caring" profession such as psychology. There are both overt and more subtle factors such as clout and compensation that can deter a male from going into the "pink collar" professions of nursing, teaching, or mental health.

Research indicates that across different mental health disciplines, there is a documented widespread lack of males in counseling and psychology training (Coffman, et al., 2018). This low representation of males reflects both a cause and an effect of the feminization of those components of mental health. Understanding the factors that facilitate or serve as barriers to men even deciding to enter an applied clinical profession will help men to get more involved.

Gender role strain refers to the mental or physical tension caused by gender role conflict related to masculine, feminine, or androgynous roles (O'Neil, 2008). Gender nonconforming, queer, and transgender people are challenging what we see as "mainstream." It's important to understand that experiencing gender role conflict or strain is when a person feels uncomfortable when behaving outside the typical societal expectations for that person's gender. Imagine attending a baby shower. One of the men present sees an outfit and exclaims, "This is just so precious, and what a darling shade of pink. I bet it'll really look adorable on the baby. It makes me wish I had a baby just for all the fun clothes!" If your reaction is "that's unusual" then that expresses gender role strain. This perception extends to factors that we've been taught that aren't especially masculine, including asking for help, working in a helping profession, communicating about feelings, and establishing deep same-sex relationships. Each sends a message that a man working in perinatal mental health is out of his element. Dan was very fortunate to find a psychologist mentor early in his professional life who modeled that it was okay for men to base a career on early fatherhood. The British Psychological Society (2016) sees the same need because it has designated men as a minority group and is actively recruiting more men to join!

Help for Men

We need a gender-equitable, whole-family approach to parental mental health. We should focus on the fact that men are roughly 50 percent of the parents who need services and attention. To accomplish this goal, maternal health therapists and organizations should evaluate the impressions they present to those seeking assistance. People seek support and information by conducting website searches. In a quick survey of provider directories on postpartum support websites, nearly all of the therapists listed are female.

Rather than asking, "Why don't the dads come in for appointments, classes, or workshops?" the question is, "Why would they?" The most common barrier is the therapist's or organization's web presence; the look and feel of a website. This approach means addressing the "peripheral characteristics" in program design. These factors refer to the messaging, the branding, and their overall appearance—which often reflects a powerful "smell test" that suggests if an organization is "for me/us" or not. In the world of perinatal mental health, the words and images on the website, the messages on social media, and the pictures on the walls in the waiting room typically exclude images of men. Fathers are usually not mentioned.

Language matters. Names such as *Women's Reproductive Behavioral Health* and *Women Helping Women* send a clear message. Another site called the *Mother-Child Institute* sounds female-centric, however, it does offer help for fathers and families. By the same token, if the waiting room at the clinic or organization doesn't have any guy-friendly magazines, or the men's room doesn't have a changing station, it sends a clear message about who the "real" patient is. The manner in which the receptionist treats dads is powerful. If he or she avoids eye contact, seems uncomfortable, or doesn't answer his questions clearly, then that avoidance presents one more barrier to involvement such as attending appointments. Additional barriers that many dads face include logistics. Paternity leave is usually short, and most clinics only schedule appointments during the day when the father is likely to be at work.

Putting into Practice: Practical Recommendations

Organizations and offices should be encouraged to:

1. Have more diversity in the magazines in their lobby
2. Open up some evening and weekend hours
3. Train their staff to be equally attentive and available to all, no matter what gender

4. Work to hire males and fathers when possible
5. Make sure to include images of fathers competently involved with their infants in their online and print marketing materials
6. Have father-specific resources and referrals to give to dads who need them

Research shows that men are less likely to seek help, especially for mental health needs (Vogel & Heath, 2016). A large survey conducted in the United Kingdom by their Mental Health Foundation found that in a poll of over 2,500 people with mental health problems, 28 percent of men compared with 19 percent of women had not sought medical help (United Kingdom Mental Health Foundation Survey, 2016). The old adages "just support your wife" and "protect and provide" help explain why so many expectant and new dads simply don't feel entitled to reach out and ask for support when things get tough. In fact, more recent research by Pew Research scientists suggests a growing trend toward seeing moms and dads as being more similar in their parenting roles and related needs for support (Pew, 2013).

Chapter 2

DADS PAST AND PRESENT

"A father is a biological necessity, but a social accident."
—MARGARET MEAD, ANTHROPOLOGIST

"The primary consequences of fatherlessness are rising male violence and declining child well-being and the underlying source of our most important social problems."
—DAVID BLANKENHORN, CO-FOUNDER OF THE NATIONAL FATHERHOOD INITIATIVE

Although the two quotes above come from popular scholars who have academic credentials, they're both basically wrong when it comes to humans. The issue is that most Western countries have social rules that teach an "essentialist" view of fatherhood. Even the most hard-core scientists begin with a cultural bias that impacts what they study and how they interpret their findings. The idea that fathers, just because they're men, make some "essential" contribution to their children's development, has been largely debunked. The same school of thought which suggests that mothers are the "essential" ingredient to the healthy psychological development of babies, infants, and toddlers has also been disproved.

> **Some common misperceptions about THE "ESSENTIAL FATHER"**
>
> 1. The biological experiences of pregnancy and lactation generate a strong, instinctual drive in women to nurture. In the absence of these experiences, men do not have an instinctual drive to nurture infants and children.
> 2. A man's contribution to reproduction is limited to conception, so active and consistent parenting by fathers is difficult for them.
> 3. Without marriage to hold them down, men will try to get as many women pregnant as possible but won't take care of the babies.
> 4. When fathers take care of young children, their unique masculine presence helps kids to be healthier, and this is especially true for boys who need a male role model.

Psychologists synthesized a wide range of cross-species, cross-cultural, and social science research to show that it's not mothers or fathers per se that are important, but that people of any gender can raise happy, healthy children (Silverstein & Auerbach, 1999). It turns out that gender by itself isn't very important in how well any one person parents even the youngest of children. Rather, the issue is what society has trained us to believe. Of course, science has shown that there are some clear physical and psychological differences between men and women—in particular with respect to expressing aggression and sexuality—but nowhere has it been shown that either gender is better or more important for the parenting of babies. Fathers and mothers are supposed to be contributing to the healthy development of our kids.

Men's and women's roles in domestic and professional worlds have changed considerably compared with fifty years ago. Nowhere is the shift in men's roles more visible than in fathers as they move beyond the traditional "protector and provider." They are becoming more highly involved with their babies and partners. In a 2016 Pew Research Center survey of adults in the U.S., nearly three quarters of respondents felt that it was equally important for new babies to bond with both parents (Pew, 2017).

Percent saying it's more important for new babies to have more time to bond with...

The traditional role of fathers has evolved through Western history. In general, fathers have been seen as taking a minor role in the care of their children, especially very young children and babies. Even today, if you ask a father-to-be during pregnancy how he sees his role, his answer translates to the traditional "protect and provide" masculine role. He will earn, discipline, put food on the table, and keep the family safe.

The roots of this model in which fathers are expected to show a high level of control over their families are clearly seen in the Puritan times of the United States. Given the typical assertion that God is a man, the Judeo-Christian ethic put men and fathers squarely in control in society, their families, and themselves. In this tradition, the paternal role parallels the fatherly relationship that God was thought to have had with Abraham, Moses, and Jesus. Disciplining children, providing resources, and serving as a moral model of values reflected the vast majority of the father's role during this period.

During the period of rapid industrialization and expansion of the mid-nineteenth century, the "breadwinner" dimension of fatherhood came to be the most central aspect of fathers' contribution to their children's well-being.

During the first half of the 20th century, the popular understanding of fathers' responsibilities came to center around fathers as a key gender role model, especially for their sons. The political and gender revolutions of the 1960s resulted in a whole new generation of Americans revisiting social norms. The role of fathers included being active and nurturing caretakers to both their children and partners. As the feminist and women's liberation movements have gradually helped women to have more representation in the modern workplace, the traditional domestic duties considered to be "women's work," including care of children and the smooth-running of "family operations," has quite naturally begun to be shared by fathers. The Great Recession of 2008 also resulted in a large number of men and women losing their jobs. In many cases during the years it may have taken to get back into paid work, they found themselves absorbing much more responsibility for their children's day-to-day caretaking than ever before. In fact, society and fathers themselves see dads as needing to be much more involved with their children and partners than any generation in history. While there are now more female CEOs and senators than ever before, there are more single and stay-at-home dads with no precedent anywhere in Western history.

While society has made significant gains toward showing respect for women working outside the home, there hasn't been a similar recognition of men who opt to focus more on fathering than on professional development. One of Dan's friends, who is a stay-at-home-dad, made this interesting comment: "Now that I've been asked by so many people why we decided to have me stay home instead of my wife, I think I can better understand the frustration and outrage that many gay dad couples feel when someone asks them an ignorant question like, 'Which one is the Mommy?'" To be fair, this social dynamic is slowly improving, and an example from popular media comes from the father-centric "man-vertising" aired during Super Bowl commercials. We see huge, buff athletes wearing tutus and having tea parties with their young daughters. It is a direct message along the lines of, "real men get over their hang-ups and risk looking silly or feminine in order to connect with their kids." This is great except that this evolution of the fatherhood role has generally not included the perinatal period. Even today, most television shows, films, and even children's books portray fathers of babies as either absent or the "bumbling dad" stereotype who puts the diaper on the baby's head and then hands a howling baby back to the all-knowing mother for proper care.

This misconception about early fathers' skills brings us back to the two quotes at the beginning of this chapter, in which two well-known social scientists suggest that fathers are either not all that important, or alternately, are absolutely essential to the psychological and social development of their children. Many years of research has shown that having a consistent, warm caregiver who is attuned to a child's needs is most important for the healthy development of children. While there is some research that shows that moms and dads do engage in parenting in somewhat different ways, there simply isn't any data that shows that one is better than the other, or that it matters if it's a mom or a dad providing the care.

Fortunately, the old "sexual-conflict-of-interest hypothesis" that indicates male mammals will maximize their evolutionary fitness by impregnating as many females as possible without contributing much to their care turns out not to be applicable to human fathers (Trivers, 1972). In fact, the "paternity hypothesis" has shown that there is actually more overlap between the sexes in parenting behavior and that human fathers, including nonbiological father figures, have what it takes to be solid parents (Smuts & Gubernick, 1992).

DAD 2.0

Compared to the old-school Dad 1.0 bullet points in Chapter 1, the Positive Psychology/Positive Masculinities (Kiselica & Englar-Carlson, 2010) approach paints a more well-rounded picture of men today.

Male Relational Styles: Fun, shared activities

Male Ways of Caring: Caring, protection, and "action empathy"

Generative Fatherhood: Developing kids

Male Self-Reliance: Connected, yet "his own man"

Workplace/Provider: Achievement, purpose, and meaning

Male Courage/Risk-Taking: Worthwhile, sensible risks

Group Orientation: Identity in community

Humanitarian Service: Social interest and common good

Humor: Healing, coping, and connecting

Male Heroism: Overcoming obstacles

This list of traits underlines a big shift in how researchers and leaders in the field see not one single form of masculinity. We now think of different masculini*ties*, which reflect the many facets of what being a man means. These characteristics are important because they address the often difficult-to-answer question, "What does it mean to be a man?" The idea isn't that a man must be all of these things all the time because that would just be another, updated "guy box." These traits are meant as a road map describing some of the best ways to be a man. Even though it's not necessary for a "real man" to be a father it's key that these researchers included "Generative Fatherhood" as one important piece of positive masculinity. In fact, the most common response Dan gets when he asks male friends, colleagues, and clients what it means to be a man boils down to being a responsible, reliable father who puts his family first. Of course, men and dads often take this selflessness too far at the expense of their own well-being, and we'll address that point in chapter six.

Generative Fatherhood

These days, the most common buzz words are "responsible fathers," "engaged fathers," "involved dads," and "generative fathers" as you see in the Positive Psychology/Positive Masculinities chart. These terms all basically mean the same thing, and the idea of generative fathering is that the dad (or father figure) shows a commitment to caring for the next generation by working to guide children and prepare them to thrive. This understanding of fatherhood draws from a popular psychological model of human development that came from Eric Erikson (1950). Erikson's model shows that one of the key life transitions that adults experience is working toward what he called "generativity." Generativity in this context means that the father comes to have an expanded sense of himself, which includes committing to and caring for the next generation. This role of preparing children for the world isn't by any means new, but the specific ways in which dads are leaning into fatherhood are definitely different from prior generations.

Paternal Involvement

Paternal "involvement" has been typically measured by whether or not the father lived in the household with the child and provided some type of financial assistance. In the last 30 years, research and policy has come to see what fathers have to offer their children—including their infants—as being much more than just living at home and providing resources for them. Building off of previous research and theory, Dan's research team has developed the Paternal Involvement with Infants Scale (Singley, et al., 2018) that gives a more nuanced multidimensional look at the ways that today's dads tend to be involved with their babies. The key dimensions that Dan's research team has identified that dads are involved in their babies' lives include:

- **Positive Engagement:** Direct caretaking
- **Warmth and Attunement:** Playing with the baby
- **Indirect Care:** Behaviors that are not directly interacting with their children, but involve arranging for the child to have important resources (e.g. taking the baby to doctor appointments or day care)
- **Frustration:** Emotional involvement or frustration with his baby
- **Control & Process Responsibility:** "Meta-involvement" in which the father monitors the other four domains and the baby's overall life

So, while you don't need to be a fatherhood researcher to understand how important it is for dads to be involved with their partners and babies, you can use the areas above as a guide to understand the different ways that fathers these days are invested in their babies.

Putting into Practice: Assessing the Fatherhood Role

One common theme that causes confusion or disagreement among dads and moms is about what the "correct" role is for new dads. Part of the confusion derives from the "fatherhood generation gap" that new dads commonly experience. They feel the need to be more engaged and involved with their babies and partners but don't have models from their own fathers or even popular media. In clinical practice it is useful to provide a list of research-based, concrete, actionable methods.

- Fostering a positive relationship with the child's mother
- Spending time with the child
- Nurturing the child
- Disciplining appropriately
- Serving as a guide to the outside world
- Protecting and providing
- Being a role model

This list comes from a United States Department of Health and Human Services report titled, *The Role of the Father in the Healthy Development of Children* (Rosenberg & Wilcox, 2006). It spells out the essential aspects of what the fatherhood role involves. It is used as a self screen for the dad's behavior and becomes a guide for improvement. Using this tool in an ongoing way, as a lifetime practice, is intended to produce positive outcomes for dads, their partners, and their children alike.

Chapter 3

DADS SUFFER TOO

S tatistically, the rates of postpartum depression are similar in fathers and mothers. We know who is at risk. It is essential to be frank about personal and family histories of mental illness. There is no shame acknowledging the truth. Stigma often prevents people from getting help.

Parental Mental Health

The field of perinatal mental health includes moms, dads, and parents of any gender, however, it's most commonly referred to as, "maternal mental health." Relatedly, people most commonly think of perinatal mental health as consisting of postpartum depression, or often just plain "postpartum." Experiencing crippling depression and devastating anxiety contrast sharply with the Hollywood version of early parenthood. This disconnect between reality and what's expected is at the heart of the stigma that often prevents moms and dads from opening up about what they're experiencing during this major life transition.

Thanks to brave celebrity moms like Brooke Shields, Chrissy Tiegen, and Serena Williams, the general public has clear examples in which new moms suffer with depression and anxiety. One in five new mothers experience postpartum depression or anxiety (Wisner, et al., 2013), and between 10 and 20 percent of new dads experience some type of depression or anxiety disorder. This is more than the typical stress or worry that accompanies new parenthood. Although both the popular media and the scientific mental health literature focus much more attention on maternal mental health, the fact is that moms and dads are much more similar than they are different in terms of how they experience the psychological shift of new parenthood.

While research studies have shown that one in ten dads develops postpartum depression (Singley & Edwards, 2015), we don't often stop to consider or ask dads the basic question: "How are you doing? No, how are you REALLY doing?" To make things even more difficult, dads' symptoms of depression are often different from the typical signs we think of such as being unable to get out of bed, crying, having no energy, and having suicidal thoughts. While dads can and do experience these aspects of depression, they will often show what's called "Masked Male Depression" (Rabinowitz & Cochran, 2008) or Major Depressive Disorder—Male type (Chuik, et al., 2009). Depressed men—including fathers—commonly show signs of extreme irritability or anger, being isolated or socially withdrawn (even if around people at home or work), an increase in drinking or drug use (or other "dopaminergic" activities like videogaming or having affairs), and physical/somatic issues like headaches or muscle tension. The socializing messages we give men like "be tough," "don't burden others with your problems," "you need to sacrifice for others," and "men can't show weaknesses" contribute specifically to how a dad will commonly experience and enact his experience of depression and/or anxiety.

Prevalence of diagnosable anxiety disorders in the prenatal period ranges from 4.1 to 16 percent, and between 2 and 18 percent postpartum. Even though we think of depression when discussing reproductive mental health difficulties, dads and couples often have more anxiety than depression.

Generalized Anxiety Disorder, Obsessive-Compulsive Disorder, and Post-Traumatic Stress Disorder are more than just the general stress and anxiety that naturally accompany the transition to parenthood. Parental mental health issues also include a prevalence of disorders, which may begin prenatally during the pregnancy. The fact is that both the joys and the concerns of the fatherhood journey begin well before the birth itself. However, it's rare that friends, family, or even medical providers will stop to check in with a dad to see if he might, indeed, be struggling before, during, or after the pregnancy. Typical dismissive comments such as, "It is what it is" and "I just let it go" or "I let it roll off my back" are phrases that we hear from dads, and they generally translate to, "It sucks and I don't know how to manage it." Because we usually don't socialize men to talk clearly and directly about their emotions, dads may speak in metaphors by saying, "I feel like I'm way out on a limb" or "I'm the safety net for my family, but I don't have one for myself." They usually mean, "I'm scared as hell, feel all alone, and don't know where to turn for help." Given that men are socialized to believe asking for help is a sign of weakness, it's no wonder that anxiety is so common throughout the beginning of the parental experience.

Maternal postpartum depression is the strongest predictor of paternal PPD. This is one of the most robust and frequently validated findings in the early fatherhood mental health literature. In heterosexual couples, when a mother experiences postpartum depression, 50 percent of the time, so does the child's father. From a public mental health perspective, this is a *huge* number. The implications for having two depressed parents are dire, and research shows that it can have a lasting impact a child's health. If a dad isn't supposed to experience depression in general, and his understanding of his role is to forego his own needs in order to support her, what are the odds that a father will reach out for help when his partner is seriously struggling? Virtually nobody teaches men, boys, or dads that their own self-care is every bit as important as their partner's. Yet a volume of research shows that when dads do stop to engage in key self-care activities such as minding their diet, exercise, sleep, and social support, then both they and their families benefit in long-lasting ways.

Maternal gatekeeping is a common postpartum experience that describes a dynamic in which the mom controls and diminishes the dad's ability to directly engage with the baby. The reality is that some dads engage in their own version of gatekeeping, although it's most frequently seen with moms (both in therapy and in the research literature in this area). This tendency to think of the parenting of infants and babies as the purview of moms means that if there are disagreements, Mom is always right, and Dad needs to get in line behind her. The basic dynamic at play is often that Dad will do some things differently than Mom does with the baby. This difference causes anxiety in Mom, and she will then manage her stress via a kind of avoidance-by-proxy. She keeps the dad from interacting with the baby in ways that she disagrees with and which cause her anxiety. The result is a spiral in which the dad resents her for not allowing him to be as involved as he wants to be. He shuts down and pulls back. In doing so, he has fewer opportunities to develop the confidence he needs to care for the baby. He will then be less inclined to help out, and so the mother is upset about the strain in the relationship as well as him not helping out. It becomes a cycle which is best addressed by talking with the couple about differing parenting styles, how to communicate when they disagree, and taking slow steady steps to challenge each other's worries. As mentioned earlier, there are of course situations in which the dad's anxiety and avoidant gatekeeping behavior need to be addressed in order for the couple to both feel heard and able to co-parent appropriately.

Men Have Hormones Too

There may be hormones that prepare men for fatherhood. Studies have shown evidence that men who are exposed to a pregnant partner have hormonal changes. Close contact may accelerate the beginning of a father's responsiveness in human and nonhuman species (Storey, et al., 2000). While the relative direction of change in hormones around the birth of their baby is the same for moms and dads, the key difference is that the magnitude of the change is larger for mothers than it is for dads. The implications of these hormonal shifts in dads isn't well understood. Does the "sympathetic weight gain" phenomenon often observed in fathers during pregnancy result from these changes? Anthropologists use the term "couvade" to describe these symptoms (Clinton, 1986). It has been observed and studied in a variety of cultures from around the world, however, the link with hormones has not been sufficiently studied (Brennan, 2014).

A large retrospective epidemiologic study of three hundred pregnancies found that 22 percent of the expectant fathers had twice the number of doctor visits while the wife was pregnant than prior to or after delivery. His complaints resulted in being prescribed medication. At no point was his wife's pregnancy noted in the medical records (Lipkin, et al., 1982).

One of the reasons the early parenthood journey is different for moms and dads is the physical/biological experience of carrying and delivering a baby. With the exception of transgender dads who are gestational parents, the nine-month experience of growing and delivering a baby is uniquely female. A common misconception, however, is that fathers can't develop perinatal depression or anxiety because they don't experience the hormonal shifts that moms do. The reality is that for people of all genders, developing parental mental health issues is related to a variety of factors, including neurobiological predispositions, family history, trauma experiences, changes to sleep patterns, increased stress and responsibilities, relationship with partners—and hormonal changes. A series of well-controlled research studies have shown that fathers do indeed show changes in their own hormones, which mirror those of moms right around the birth of their baby (Gettler, et al., 2011; Kuo, et al., 2018):

- Decrease in testosterone
- Increase in cortisol
- Increase in estrogen (estradiol)
- Increase in prolactin/oxytocin

Recent research has begun to draw a link between hormone levels in dads with postpartum depression, showing that decreased testosterone in new dads predicted depression at two and nine months postpartum (Saxbe, et al., 2017). There needs to be more rigorous research on the hormonal changes in men around the birth of their babies. While the emphasis on the biochemical shifts for females is logical, it has minimalized the male experience. It is important to explore the biological intricacies of all genders.

Expectations versus Realities

Previous chapters have described the experiences and expectations of new dads. Whether your expectation is to be a "super dad" who wants to be highly involved in every aspect of the pregnancy, birth, and caring for the newborn, or a more hands-off type of father who's content to go to work and handle the overflow when your partner feels overwhelmed, early fatherhood is often a different experience than many expect it will be. Independent of their professional or working backgrounds, men and dads tend to share a common approach in planning for what will happen in the future. What they expect when becoming a dad will likely differ in significant ways from what they have seen in previous generations with their own families, and even from their friends.

Gender Similarities Hypothesis

As gender roles continue to evolve, we're seeing men and women do things somewhat differently than in the past, which can look a bit confusing to those who are used to a more traditional division of new parent labor. New dads often explain their feelings of being unneeded for baby-centric assignments by saying, "She's got the boobs, and all the baby does is sleep, eat, and poop, so I feel like there's not much for me to do until the kid's older." Another similar point may be, "I'm the hunter and she's the nurturer/gatherer, so I need to be out there earning, and she's better at taking care of the baby." Yes, of course, men are hardware-challenged and don't breastfeed babies (although trans-dads can chest-feed them!), but there is no behavioral genetic research that supports the idea that women are naturally better parents to infants than men. In fact, the findings from this area of research generally show that neither moms nor dads are "better" or more essential. It turns out that gender really doesn't make one parent better or worse when it comes to raising happy and healthy babies. Contrary to the *Men are from Mars and Women are from Venus* point of view, the research on gender has consistently shown that men and women are actually much more psychologically similar than they are different, with the general finding that men and women are about 70 percent the same in terms of psychosocial functioning (Hyde, 2005). As shown in this chart, you can see that when you take a normal curve of men's psychosocial attributes and superimpose it over a similar curve for women, the genders are far more similar than they are different:

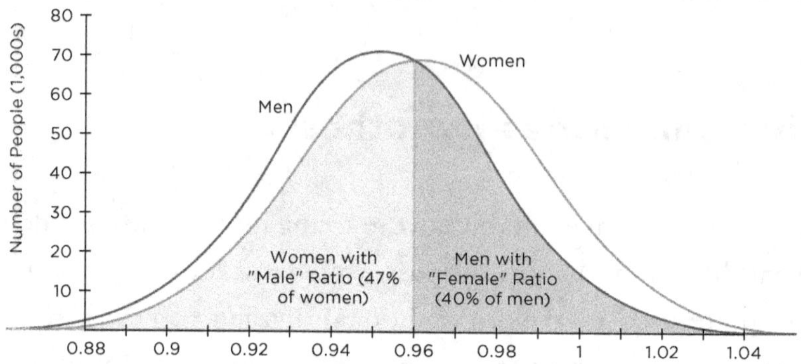

Putting into Practice: Training Implications

Although women and men have a lot in common in terms of their ability to be good parents, as a society we haven't devoted equal time and energy to understand how to support fathers' transition into parenthood. Some findings from researchers who have begun to draw attention to dads' needs have shed light on how their partners, friends, mental health providers, and peer supporters alike can better understand some of the most common areas of need that new dads experience—in particular, those dads who develop symptoms of depression. The list below comes from a qualitative study in which the researchers interviewed new dads with postpartum depression and asked them to talk about what aspects of their mental health difficulties was most central to them (Eddy, et al., 2019):

- Needing education
- Address gender expectations
- Repressing feelings
- Being overwhelmed
- Resentment
- Experience of neglect

This list points to some simple yet important ways that we can support dads. The first is to provide them with the knowledge they need about the facts of their own mental health. Imagine how many fewer dads would suffer if they heard during prenatal classes that there is a 10 percent chance that they'll develop depression and up to an 18 percent chance that they'll experience an anxiety disorder in the first year of parenthood? In the same way that we often avoid discussing mental health concerns, the field of "maternal" mental health doesn't really lend itself to including masculinity. The role transition to fatherhood is an important part of the wellness narrative, and dads in this study clearly indicated that their partners' and their own expectations of "being a man" played a huge part in their depression. While a lot of new parents feel overwhelmed, learning to "stuff" difficult stressful feelings is a classic aspect of old school, rigid masculinity, and the dads who reflected on their postpartum depression saw this unhealthy attempt at coping as being key in causing and maintaining their depression.

Dads have expressed feeling invisible in prenatal classes, during the birth process, at well baby visits, and even with their own extended families throughout the perinatal period. At a time when dads expect to be much more involved, it's understandable that in working to get in there to play a major role, that they find themselves feeling resentful when important players in the process don't recognize them that way or put up barriers to their involvement.

The Expectant Dad's Birth Plan

It's common for pregnant parents to develop a birth plan that they share with their birthing professional to clarify the specifics of how they're hoping the birth will go. Factors such as whether to use pain medication, have a Cesarean birth, use a doula, and have the infant vaccinated are often parts of this plan. Unfortunately, the dads all too often are surprised by or don't have a voice in the planning. While of course it's the woman's body that's giving birth, and therefore her choice about what happens to her and her body, dads have felt completely blindsided—and in some cases traumatized—by experiences that occurred during even a completely uncomplicated vaginal birth. Dads can play an important role in the birth planning process by initially interviewing their partners to find out their preferences and then documenting them to share with their birthing professional. It's essential to understand that the formal birth plan is just "Plan A." Dads can prepare themselves and their partners for the birth by exploring what they'll do item-by-item if, for some reason, they can't have that aspect of their plan. Active labor is not a good time to be trying to take in new information and make big decisions. Together, moms and dads benefit from preparing themselves by collaborating about the birth plan.

Another factor in birth planning is for the dad's partner to honor his role in the big day by interviewing him about his own preferences. Again, the idea isn't at all that he's exerting control over the mother or her body, but it's important for his partner to understand how he sees her involvement and what he's wishing for even though it isn't his decision when it comes down to the mechanics of the actual birth. Partners are encouraged to get dads into the birth game by asking him these questions while the mother also voices her own preferences: (Adapted from the American Pregnancy Association)

- Who do you want to be present?
- Do you want a doula?
- Will there be children/siblings present?
- Do you want to be "downtown" to receive your baby, or prefer to be "uptown" by your partner's head?

- What will your partner likely do for pain relief? (massage, hot and cold packs, positions, labor imagery, relaxation, breathing exercises, tub or Jacuzzi, medication)
- How do you feel about fetal monitoring?
- What do you plan to be eating and drinking?
- How do you feel about pain medications or other procedures including an episiotomy? Or, are there certain measures you're concerned about?
- What are your preferences for your baby's care? (when to feed, where to sleep)
- For home and birth center births, what are your plans for hospital transport in case of emergency?
- If you need a cesarean, do you have any special requests? Have you ever been in an operating room?

Remember that this isn't an invitation for conflict or trying to force each other into agreement. It's about giving dads a way to voice their needs, hopes, and boundaries—it's okay to disagree! What's most important is to know ahead of time the other partner's hopes so you can communicate and work to find the middle ground proactively as needed. Doing so really helps to get the dad's "head into the game" by having him clearly imagine the birth process and to have a voice in it.

Putting into Practice: Postpartum Game Plan

Expectant couples are encouraged to ask the following questions during the second or third trimester of pregnancy. The idea is for both of them to voice their thoughts, which reflect important boundaries, and to facilitate conversation. The key part of the unfolding process is to recognize and acknowledge their own and each other's feelings—NOT to try to force agreement.

1. What resources will you need if you should have to stay in the neo-natal intensive care unit?
2. How long do you anticipate needing to recover after the birth?
3. When is the soonest that friends or family can meet your baby after the birth?
4. When is the soonest that friends or family can come to your house after the birth?
5. Will any friends or family be staying with you in your home during the first three to four months after birth? If so, what are your expectations for them?
6. If you work, how long will you be taking off before going back?
7. Do you need to do any legal or estate planning activities (setting up/revising wills, trusts)?
8. What if any childcare services will you need, and when?
9. Are you planning to use a doula, night nanny, or other type of postpartum consultant?
10. When do you expect to resume activities such as going out to eat, attending movies, meeting with friends?
11. When is the soonest that you expect dad to be able to spend time alone with baby?
12. What are some ways that friends and family can help you out in the first few months after birth?
13. How will you arrange to have regular "couple time" to connect and check in with each other (without doing "family business")?
14. Do you plan to breast feed, bottle-feed, or both? Mothers milk, formula, or both?
15. How much of the daily care (feeding, burping, swaddling, diapering, bathing, doctor visits, soothing) will you be doing, and are there any of them that will be particularly easy or difficult for you?
16. Where will baby sleep?
17. How will you be handling feeding and care of your newborn at night?

18. If baby will be sleeping in your room, how long until you move her/him to another room?

19. When do you anticipate that your baby will be able to sleep through the night, and what, if anything, do you plan to do to help her/him to sleep as long as possible?

20. Which family and friends would be the most helpful if you need help?

21. Who would be some people that might "second-guess" your parenting, or who might not respect your boundaries?

22. When do you anticipate resuming sex?

23. What kinds of nonsexual physical intimacy/gestures do you want to make sure continue?

24. Name two people—other than your partner—who you can connect with in person to get some social support during the first few months postpartum? How will you reach out to them? What might prevent you from getting this much-needed support?

25. What are a couple of activities that you will do to "recharge your batteries" on a regular basis?

26. If you are feeling stressed or overwhelmed, how would you express it and to whom?

27. Would you have any difficulty letting your partner know if you experience common concerns (anxiety, sadness, guilt, jealousy, resentment, frustration, anger) related to your new role as a parent?

28. If you have had any mental health difficulties in the past, what resources (therapist, medication, books, websites) would be most helpful to you should you need them?

Chapter 4

DON'T BE A BYSTANDER

Social and emotional support are critical while a pregnant couple is transitioning from being a duo to parenthood. As individuals and together, they are entering a new phase of life. This journey is scary as well as exciting for moms and dads alike. They are facing challenges, decisions, and fears. Pregnancy is a time to have conversations. Who will provide a safe environment where both the man and woman can talk, cry, and not be judged? As previously stated, the maternal mental health movement is female-centric, both socially and clinically. While peer support groups have been available, they usually focus on motherhood and leave the father feeling excluded, ignored, and neglected. Dads also need education and a safe place to talk about their feelings, being overwhelmed, and perhaps resentful.

Many years of research have shown that right about the time when parents are beginning to have their children, their sense of satisfaction with their relationship is likely to be taking a dip (Frisco & Williams, 2003). Different studies vary in terms of the timeframe in which couples will experience the deepest part of this dip, but statistically, new parents will be likely to have some struggles with their relationship that accompany their journey into new parenthood. After a period of years, their relationship satisfaction picks back up, and the couple is happier together. This data is a combination of many thousands of people and multiple studies. Of course, rather than follow a U-shaped curve, some couples will remain highly happy, others will stay at a consistent low level of satisfaction, others will just go from low to high, and others from high to low. This information may be scary to expectant and new parents, but it is important not to go "on autopilot." How we communicate in marriage highlights how we teach boys, men, and dads to express their own needs and feelings.

U-Shaped Curve of Marital Happiness

Emotional and Physical Intimacy

In general, emotional and physical intimacy are linked for romantic couples. If they feel very emotionally connected, they also tend to have a more satisfying sex life. By the same token, couples who experience a lot of physical intimacy—not just sex—often feel emotionally connected with each other. Each of these two dimensions of intimacy can lead to the other. Examples of nonsexual physical intimacy include holding hands, hugging, sitting together with your legs touching on the sofa, back rubs, and kissing.

There are factors that result in new parents experiencing a disruption in their sex lives, including stopping engaging in these nonsexual types of physical intimacy. An individual will have their own unique constellation of issues that will cause their sex lives to change compared to antenatally and before getting pregnant. A few of these factors include having a baby in your room, losing sleep, feeling tired all the time, having family members in the house, feeling unattractive, recovery from a difficult birth, pelvic floor injury, and having postpartum mental health issues.

Experiencing changes in physical intimacy is pretty much baked into the transition to new parenthood, and there are a variety of assumptions that go along with these common changes. For example, the old sexist myth that, "women need a reason to have sex, but men just need a place" really overlooks the fact that sex is often every bit as emotional and mental for men as it is for women. We've seen a variety of ways in which sex can become complicated for men and dads. These include fertility challenges, being witness to a traumatic birth with lots of tearing, and simply experiencing a high level of jealousy. He may see his place with his partner being "taken over" by a new baby with needs that are pushing his own to the back of the line. Instead of assuming that dads are "just horny" or sexually frustrated, it's key to learn how to talk with dads about their hopes, needs, fears, and concerns about their emotional *and* physical intimacy.

One interesting area of research looks at how parents' division of household labor—including caring for children—relates to their sexual intimacy and the quality of their relationship. Moms and dads alike are increasingly expected to take more similar roles in raising their children. According to the research by Kornich, Brines, & Leupp (2013), couples report a better sense of fairness and satisfaction when household chores are shared. There is research showing that a more egalitarian arrangement in which both parents are roughly equal in sharing the domestic and financial responsibilities experience fewer problems in their satisfaction with their relationship and sexual intimacy (Frisco & Williams 2003). The findings from this 2003 study suggested that women's perceptions that the division of household labor is unfair not only decrease their own marital quality but also lead to role strain that makes them more likely to end marriages they find unsatisfying. This research is based on re-analyzing data that is twenty to thirty years old, and often doesn't directly include how the parents share the specific duties of raising children. A newer study addressed the question of egalitarian parenting roles, sex relations, and relationship satisfaction, and found that, "men's performance of childcare is generally associated with more satisfaction with the division of childcare, more satisfying sexual relationships, and higher quality relationships." These authors' findings also showed that having more equal roles in terms of parenting children had more positive consequences for moms and dads alike (Carlson, Hanson, & Fitzroy, 2016).

A wealth of information supports the fact that when partners communicate regularly, proactively, and in a balanced way about their relationship, they're much more likely to have higher levels of intimacy, connection, and satisfaction. John and Julie Gottman have done pioneering work that addresses how partners can maintain and fall out of love, and the following is a technique that we have adapted from their work on what they call the "State of the Union" meeting (Gottman & Silver, 2015). No matter what's going on with the couple, any relationship is likely to benefit from putting this approach into action.

Putting into Practice: Summit Meetings

A Summit Meeting is for both partners to better understand (not necessarily agree with) the other's experience of their relationship. The focus of a

Summit Meeting is to hold a brief (it can be as quick as five minutes—ten minutes is a very long one!) regular weekly conversation in which both partners clearly communicate to each other their own thoughts. While it may be important to circle back, problem-solve, and accept the others' influence down the line, it's critical that you and your partner actively listen to each other and put aside "fixes" during the Summit Meeting.

The brass tacks of the Summit Meeting involve clarifying to each other your own honest perspectives about the current state of your union/relationship by telling your partner your answers to the following three questions in this order:

1. What is something that's going well in our relationship?
2. What is something I'm having difficulty within our relationship?
3. What is something that you (i.e. you're telling your partner about what s/he has done) have done recently that helped me to feel loved/cared for/connected?

The following actions will devalue the Summit Meeting—so don't do them:

- Bring up issues older than a week or so—focus on the *current* state of your relationship
- Try to "fix" the issues discussed or to set goals to do anything differently (yet)
- Get defensive, make excuses, or invalidate each other—just listen and work to understand
- Skip telling each other about the second point above regarding difficulties you're having, no matter how small they might seem

Many people, especially partners in a relationship who either have high levels of conflict or who actively avoid any conflict at all, find the prospect of using this technique to be daunting. But remember that Einstein's definition of insanity was trying the same thing over and over while expecting a different result. Most couples find the Summit Meeting to be anxiety-provoking, formulaic, or even a bit messy the first three or four times, but by the fifth time, they're usually looking forward to it. Give yourselves *at least six hours* to reflect after the Summit Meeting before you discuss feedback, changes, or fixes to make related to issues discussed in the meeting. A wealth of research in this area shows that couples who regularly communicate proactively and respectfully about their feelings in the relationship tend to have the highest levels of satisfaction and lower levels of damaging/unproductive conflict.

Creating Affirming Social Networks

There is a lot of evidence that social support and community networks are protective factors for good mental health (World Health Organization, 2004). All new families should ideally have access to peer support in their own communities. The American Psychiatric Association approved a Position Statement on Peer Support Services saying that, "Peer support offers advantages in outreach and engagement, provision of hope, coaching and modeling, recovery skill building, and system navigation." (APA, 2018)

In the 1970s, Jane was involved with creating a postpartum parent support organization in her own community. It was founded to respond to the emotional needs of pregnant and postpartum men and women. Their organization was conceived from their own needs as struggling young parents, away from their families, and inundated with professional advice. The childbirth education movement had already begun. The expectation was that fathers, for the first time, could be included in labor and delivery rooms. They all felt equally invested, ignorant, and without parenting skills. The feminist expectation was that there would be no distinction between male or female parenting based on gender. What they lacked was a supportive environment where they could share highs and lows each week and not be judged or criticized when admitting to feeling overwhelmed, scared, or inadequate. The organization provided peer social support. It was about making friends, learning about community resources, how to ask for professional help, and gaining confidence as new parents. They wanted to have conversations as couples. If professional help was needed, there would be no stigma associated with requesting a referral.

There are four types social support. The first type of support is called practical or instrumental help. The second is emotional support, which includes encouragement, affection, approval, and feelings of "together-ness." Informational support includes sharing advice, answering questions, as well as facilitating active problem solving. The fourth type is comparison support and comes when encouragement, advice, or information are shared between individuals with similar or the same situations (Davis, Logsdon & Birkmer 1996).

Social support has both genetic and environmental variables. It is about who we are, how we interact with others, and external stressors. It includes accepting who we are, as well as giving, getting, and giving back again. It covers three domains: 1.) the extent to which individuals are attached to others, 2.) the individual's cognitive appraisal of the support, and 3.) the response of others in the provision of support (WHO, 2004).

It is a challenge to create and sustain parent peer support networks that are equitable. The majority of existing groups focus only on mothers. It is a significant challenge to change this cultural bias. To do so will require a concerted effort by men and women and means affirming that parents have equal needs, rights, and responsibilities.

Having a baby is hard on relationships and marriage. Statistics challenge the hope that the addition of a baby will preserve or even improve partnerships. Couples may let their relationship go on "autopilot" and have conflict in reactive and unproductive ways before having children. Once they have a child or are preparing to have one, their relationship can become dominated by all things baby related. There are a variety of ways that dads can feel swept to the side into a kind of bystander role. Research and common sense show that everyone benefits when dads, partners, friends, peers, mental health clinicians, and the community work to keep fathers in more central and active positions as parents and teammates. It is useful to remember that a good relationship is essential and communicating as a couple should come first. One key element of assertive communication is to connect proactively about how the relationship is going, rather than waiting to do so reactively when there are problems. By keeping ahead of issues, even small ones, couples can develop a pressure relief valve that can prevent resentments from building up and festering over time. The following tips for having more effective assertive communication are adapted from information in David Burns' 1989 book on cognitive-behavioral therapy, *The Feeling Good Handbook*.

Putting into Practice: Assertive Communication

In order to communicate as effectively as possible—especially during conflict—it's important to learn how to break old habits of escalating or checking out. Conflict is a necessary part of any relationship. The key is to make conflict productive by keeping it under control and working to create as much understanding as possible. Communication styles exist on a continuum with passive on one end, aggressive on the other, and assertive right in the middle:

Aggressive	Assertive	Passive
Only MY needs matter	BOTH of our needs matter	Only YOUR needs matter

The core of assertive communication is to first work to understand the other person's point. The first step is to quit trying to win or escape. Focus on working to understand the other person's point of view *in great detail.* Only then should you work to clarify your point to her/him. Avoid "fixing" or identifying next steps. Showing that you care enough to understand the other person's perspective is "doing" something and is the best way to express your own perspective so that s/he is likely to hear and understand you.

You do this by using a few concrete techniques:

1. Lead with Wanting to Understand the Other Person

Open questions: Ask the person a series of questions to better understand her/his position in detail. Open questions can't be answered with a simple "yes" or "no." Don't ask sarcastic or leading ones that are contemptuous or suggest what the other person needs to do. It can be very helpful to ask questions about how the current situations relate to others in her/his life (potentially in the past). The bottom line is that you need to understand specifically why this is so important to the person. Take nothing for granted (no mind reading!). Ask a minimum of three to four questions.

Restatements: Once you've asked the open question and you've heard the other person's response, restate what you heard back. "Okay, so it sounds like you're saying…" This helps the other person to feel heard, but also allows her/him to correct you as needed. Only then, once it's clear that the other person feels understood, do you continue.

2. Following Up with Wanting to be Understood

Now, it's your turn to explain your perspective. Do not argue for (nor try to persuade your partner of) your point of view; just explain how you see things. You want to be understood even if s/he doesn't agree with you. First, tell the other person all of your feelings (emotions, not thoughts) and then clarify your thoughts on the issue, and work to express how this specific issue relates to other experiences you've had in the past, your values, other people, experiences as a child/in your family of origin. Ideally, s/he is asking you open questions and making restatements, but it's possible that s/he might not know to do so. It can be helpful to ask that the other person ask you questions and restate what s/he heard.

> **Don't try to solve the problem—YET**
>
> It's much too soon to solve it. You first need to end the opposition and become each other's friend instead of foe. Be interested. Try to understand the meaning of the other person's point of view. The goal is to move from gridlock to dialogue and to understand—in depth—the other's position. You don't want a relationship in which you always win and are influential while crushing the other person. You want a relationship in which you support each other, and by understanding each other more deeply, you're very likely to find the common ground that wasn't evident to begin with.

Chapter 5

THE CORD'S CUT. NOW WHAT?

We focus now on one of the most central and enduring issues that new parents experience—how to balance work and personal life. While the professional, domestic, and overall work-life balance pictures are far from the same for mothers and fathers, the general trend is toward women assuming a larger role in the workplace, and dads spending more time with their families than ever before (Pew, 2015).

The graph on the following page represents a complicated picture. It reflects the strains that parents are feeling as they try to navigate changing personal and professional roles. As households with a full-time working father and a mother not engaged in paid work have shrunk by 20% since 1970, the number of households in which both parents are engaged in full-time paid work has increased by 15%. Importantly, as women have become much more highly involved in the workforce, the caregiving duties traditionally assigned to mothers haven't disappeared—they're becoming the shared responsibility of fathers.

In Nearly Half of Two-Parent Households, Both Mom and Dad Work Full Time

% of couples, by work arrangement

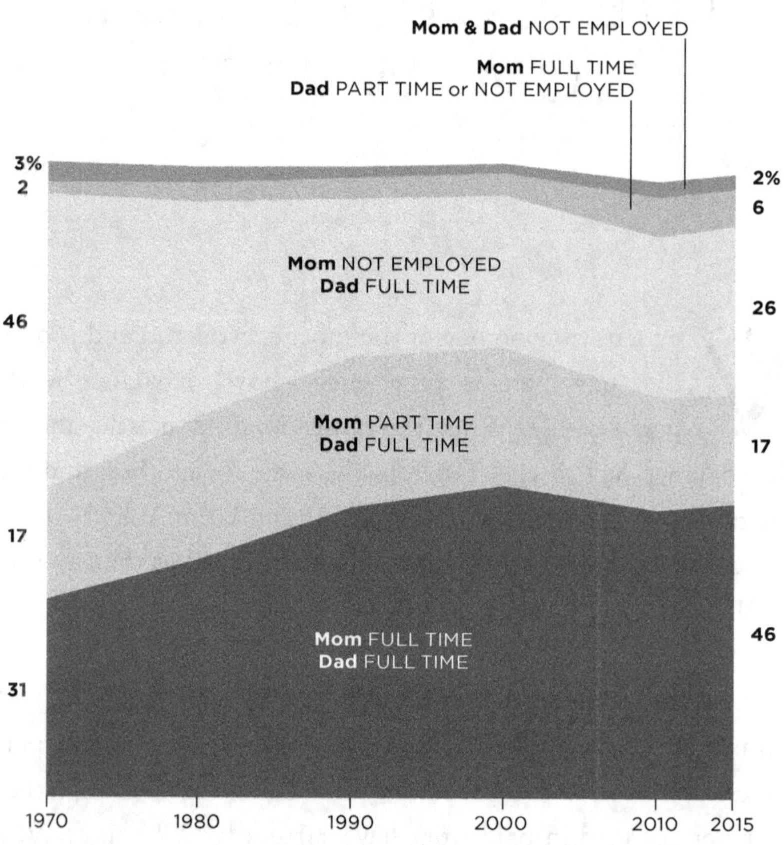

Note: Based on employment status in the prior year among male/female married couples with at least one child younder than 18 in the household. Both married and cohabitating couples included since 2010. Data regarding cohabitating couples unavailable for earlier years. Other work arrangements not shown; same-sex couples are excluded.

Source: Pew Research Center analysis of March Current Population Surveys Integrated Public Use Microdata Series (IPUMS-CPS), 1970–2015

PEW RESEARCH CENTER

A related significant issue is that relative to virtually every other developed nation in the world, the United States does a poor job of offering paid time off to moms and dads after the birth of a child, for example:

- Average maternal leave: 11 weeks
- Average paternal leave: 1 week
- 49 percent say employers put more pressure on fathers to return to work quickly versus 18 percent for mothers
- One-third say it is equal for both parents

This problem is slowly improving as some prominent companies are drawing attention to the need for moms *and* dads to take the time they need to be with their children. The dynamic is such that the dad's company technically offers a certain number of weeks of time off (usually unpaid once he has used up his paid time off), but the culture in his workplace often doesn't support his being out of the office for five to six weeks with his new baby. As an example, men in the rapidly-evolving technology fields are often afraid to take off six weeks. The perception is, "If we can get along without you for six weeks, do we really need you?" Of course, this issue also impacts moms as well, but the gender and workplace dynamics tend to be different because we are socialized to accommodate mothers putting their work on hold to focus on child-rearing.

The "New" New Dads

"Dads are reconstructing the fathering role into a new parenting paradigm that is more psychologically gratifying in the context of contemporary societal expectations."

—SILVERSTEIN, AUERBACH, & LEVANT, 2002

The quotation on the previous page means that dads are figuring out how to be authentic in light of the changing expectations of men. This is relevant because we're not used to thinking of men per se as a group that needs support. Although there are many exceptions when you factor in different groups (e.g. African-American, Latinx, LGBTQIA, religious minorities, disabled dads), because men generally experience a higher level of power and privilege relative to women, it's not all that common to think about men as a group that struggles psychologically, especially with something as basic as becoming a father. Dads are indeed struggling. They are managing the need to be more engaged fathers while shouldering professional duties without historical precedent or current models to show them the way. Even though making mistakes is part of any learning process, new parents put a lot of pressure on themselves. Bumbling along with so much uncertainty can mean that when a plate inevitably hits the floor, it feels like the end of the world. For example, "I'm the only one who struggles like this."

Moms' "Mental Load" and The Second Shift

As gender roles continue to shift, dads and moms are increasingly having to accept the reality—in many cases, the necessity—of being a dual-income household. Once a mother's place in the professional world is recognized, the father's role in domestic duties and caregiving should naturally follow. Far from being "under attack," masculinity and femininity are actually under construction in a way that is ending the assumption that domestic duties and childcare are "women's work" and legitimizing dads as caregivers.

Another important current social phenomenon is what's being called the "mental load" that many moms (and in some cases dads) are dealing with. Mental load is a situation in which moms are, as a default, assumed to be the person who "rules the roost" at home and is basically a project manager. This dynamic is based in traditional gender roles in which women are assumed to be more biologically capable with domestic duties, an assumption that has no basis in fact. Dad may be more than willing to help out with laundry, caring for the baby, and cleaning up, but he doesn't just jump in to do it on his own. He sees himself as being a good teammate because he does whatever his partner asks him to do. On the other hand, the new mother gets tired of having to be the project manager who tells him what to do. She sees a truly equal partner as someone who has just as much awareness and participation about what needs to be done as she does. In many cases, the couple finds themselves experiencing ongoing conflict at what they perceive to be their partner's unrealistic or rigid expectations. Thankfully, it usually just takes assertive communication and some consistent scheduling and planning to resolve the bulk of the issue (see the Family Logistic Meeting exercise on the next page).

A related issue is the "second shift." This term refers to what happens when a parent (mom or dad) who works outside the home, comes home to the parent who has stayed at home to care for the baby and house. The expectation is to take over parenting and domestic duties on top of the work that he or she did all day. The popular media has focused more on moms' experience of the second shift phenomenon, but with dads assuming more of the responsibility for childcare, including staying home while his partner works, dads can have a similar difficulty. Importantly, even while dads are being expected to do more with their infants and babies, there doesn't seem to be as great of an increase in how much they're expected to take part in directing the other domestic duties like cooking, cleaning, setting appointments, and transportation.

The simplest and most direct step toward managing the difficulties that surface due to mental load and the second shift are for the couple to be willing to talk openly, directly, proactively, and flexibly about the underlying issues as well as the fixes.

Putting into Practice: Family Logistics Meeting

It's important for couples to sense that they're working together as a partnership. The general pressures and stresses of daily life can pile up and result in each member of the pair feeling like s/he isn't getting the support they need. A weekly family logistics meeting (FLM) gives new parents a structure to work as a team while also making sure that they both address critical aspects of self-care. The following is adapted from Hausner and Freeman's *The Legacy Family* (2009) and Dinkmeyer and McKay's *Systematic Training for Effective Parenting* (1976).

The three key components of the Family Logistics Meeting are:

1.   A shared calendar
2.   A day-by-day review of the events in the coming seven days
3.   Adding in self-care activities

Shared Calendar

You and your partner need to have a way to coordinate your activities. The format can be a digital iCalendar, a shared Google calendar, or a plain old white board in the kitchen. If you don't yet have one, then setting up something that you can both use is the necessary first step in this process. No need to get fancy but having a shared calendar system helps you work off the same page. You both need to be consistent in adding events to the calendar so that it reflects what you actually have to get done. You do NOT need to jam it full—just include the important tasks and appointments.

Day-By-Day Review

Once your calendar is set up and you are adding events to it, you and your partner need to set a regular weekly time to review the specifics of the coming seven days. Go day-by-day to clarify each of your perspectives about who needs to be where, when, and what the related resources are to get it done. Yes, you need to do this every week. If one or both of you is grouchy, tired, or traveling, you *still* need to do it. If not a face-to-face discussion, then get on the phone, text, meet via Skype, or whatever it takes. The meeting will get you both feeling more connected and staying ahead of any surprises. We all know that the best-laid plans can get interrupted, so you'll inevitably need to be flexible because plans will change. The point here is that you'll both be on the same page about what the intended plan is, and you can revise it as needed.

Self-Care

You both need to make time to keep yourselves healthy. Once you've completed the day-by-day review, circle back and add into your schedule the times and ways in which you'll be engaging in the following three critical aspects of self-care:

- Exercise
- Social Support
- Personal Recharge Time

In addition to the points above, do not:

- Try to fill in every single block of time in your day; have flexibility
- Criticize or invalidate the other's self-care regimen
- Get "too busy" to do the logistics meeting; that's when you need it most

Expect the first couple of meetings to be a little awkward, but this is a best practice in couples—teamwork!

Chapter 6

THRIVE

The information in this section about self-care in the perinatal period isn't by any means definitive. These four pillars of self-care along with the summit and family logistics meetings help give new dads a concrete framework to guide important aspects of self-care. Fathers do need to take care of themselves as well as their baby and partner. Fathers and mothers need to sleep, eat well, exercise, have time for themselves, share their emotions, and get support. Pregnancy and the postpartum period wreck routines. It is not easy to accept help, but it is a foundation for successful parenting and well-being.

Common advice that most dads receive during pregnancy, birth, and early postpartum is, "You need to support your pregnant wife/girlfriend/partner." While of course that's a very important aspect of a new dad's role, it's just half the story. The reality is that fathers also need support during this huge change in their lives. In fact, they generally need more support than their partners, or any one person, can provide for them. Part of the problem is that when friends, family, nurses, doctors, and even mental health providers give dads the message that they should ignore their own needs in favor of their partners, they are unfortunately reinforcing the common masculine stereotype that men need to exclusively protect and provide for their loved ones while sacrificing their own needs.

Research shows that both moms and dads benefit from being proactive about focusing on their self-care during the transition to parenthood. There's no real evidence to indicate that moms need more or different psychological support than dads do. With the rapid-fire changes that occur with even a completely normal birth without any major complications, parents very commonly put all of their focus on learning how to care for their baby. They ignore how to care for themselves and each other. The bottom line is that moms and dads alike need help to be proactive about doing what it takes to keep themselves healthy during one of the biggest transitions in life.

The four key pillars of self-care are gender neutral. They are:

- Sleep
- Diet
- Exercise
- Social Support

Sleep

Most dads are told about the change in their sleep schedule that having a newborn inevitably brings. Babies vary in terms of how much and how well they sleep. Dads are also very different in terms of how much sleep they need as well as how they do with limited sleep. The most common advice that people give new parents about sleep is, "Sleep when the baby sleeps." There really is no one-size-fits-all approach to any aspect of new parenthood. It's important to recognize that part of "learning on the job" means trying out new techniques and applying what works. Key tips of sleep hygiene are:

- Have a consistent bedtime
- No sound in the bedroom except some white noise
- No blue light from devices right before bed
- Bed is only for sleeping and sex
- No caffeine, alcohol, or illicit drugs
- Use meditation or journaling to manage stressful/anxious thoughts

Imagine the bedroom of typical new parents: A bassinet next to the bed, a co-sleeper in the bed, a changing station in the corner. Anyone who has cared for a newborn will confirm that sleep tips can be pretty tough to manage in a consistent way. With a baby waking up every two to three hours and dealing with the common stress and anxiety of new parenthood, getting solid sleep can indeed be a tall order. How parents handle the nighttime routine is a very personal choice. It ranges from the "When I'm up, we're both up" approach to splitting the nighttime "shifts" to hiring a postpartum night nanny (doula) who can allow both parents to get much-needed sleep. Sleep deprivation can come from getting too little sleep as well as from consistent interruptions, which don't allow the person to get the deep, restorative sleep that is needed to feel rested. Frequent symptoms of sleep deficit include low energy, irritability, problems concentrating, anxiety, and in extreme cases, hallucinations. Especially for parents who may have a history of psychosis or mood regulation issues like bipolar depression, planning ahead and staying on top of getting ample sleep is a critical issue. The most important point is to be aware if you or your partner is running a sleep deficit. Be aware that both moms and dads need support if they are struggling with sleep.

Diet

New parents have limited time to eat a nice balanced diet (in keeping with the USDA food MyPlate) and it can be one of the first things to go. Expectant parents can focus their prenatal "nesting" time to prepare tasty/healthy frozen meals that they can use once the baby has arrived and they're still trying to figure out their new routine. Invite friends to bring meals over to the new parents. The key is to avoid snacking on whatever is convenient or relying on unhealthy "comfort foods" to manage stress. Although dads often do experience pregnancy and postpartum "sympathetic weight gain," there's nothing inevitable about gaining weight. Even the most food-conscious dad can go on autopilot and grab whatever's around instead of eating healthy foods.

We encourage dads to tell those people who ask if they can help, to take them up on the offer and have them bring over some food, do the dishes, or fold laundry. If people want to help, let them. Think about how you've felt when people you care about are in need and allow you to help them. It's generally a good feeling and you're honored to be there for the person in need. Many dads get caught up in the "rugged individualist" and protector/provider stereotypes. They will tell well-meaning friends and family who ask how they can help, "No, we're all good." Meanwhile, there's no healthy food in the house, the dishes and laundry are not done, and you're running out of diapers. But of course, their Instagram pics make it look like everything is sunshine and roses. Instead of working to maintain the illusion that you've got everything under control, give your loved ones and buddies the chance to have that same warm fuzzy feeling by taking them up on their offer to help.

Exercise

Many years of research show that getting moderate exercise is super healthy for immune functioning, cardiovascular heart health, higher life satisfaction, less stress/anxiety, and decreasing symptoms of depression. Before a baby arrives, it's common to have an active lifestyle that includes regular physical exercise, and these activities can take up a good chunk of your time. When the baby comes and the new parents are working to figure out their new routine and family logistics, their own exercise and physical well-being focus often goes on hold. That's completely understandable, but whenever possible, new and expectant parents need to think about how they can incorporate the baby into their existing lives rather than make their entire lives about the baby. There are those who may be accustomed to an exercise regimen that includes miles of running, yoga classes, playing many holes of golf, or going to the gym for hours. The issue is that it can be difficult to make space for these types of activities when you're keeping to a schedule of nursing, changing, and napping that goes on a two- to three-hour interval.

Often, what makes folks so passionate and satisfied about their hobbies or exercise is that they have high standards. They like to push themselves and get a real sense of satisfaction at continually raising the bar on their skills or stamina. It becomes a black-or-white perspective about exercise. While that mindset can indeed be very motivating, the problem with an "all or nothing" approach is that aspects of self-care are on a continuum. A sense of guilt is common and understandable. Parents need to understand that they both have important self-care needs that aren't simply just "nice to have." They are "must have" needs. In many cases, new dads don't feel confident or entitled to talk with their partners about how to take a balanced approach to help them both get out and exercise. The two factors of guilt and rigid "black-or-white" standards about what "real" exercise is can explain why many new dads put their much-needed exercise on the back-burner, often unconsciously.

The trick is to focus on balance, moderation, and consistency. The bottom line is that moderate exercise does include tucking the baby into a stroller and going for a brisk twenty-minute walk, or a short run. Anything is better than nothing at all. A dad and his partner might be isolating themselves and not tending to their physical well-being. Unless there's a medical reason not to, parents must adjust their routine and their psychological outlook to factor in how they can both go from "nothing to something" in terms of exercise. This means doing a yoga video at home, going for a quick thirty-minute run instead of doing ten miles, or heading to the gym for a quick class instead of three hours. Each of these options is far healthier than doing nothing.

Social Support

Even the most introverted person needs to have a few different sources of social support. Developing lasting, satisfying social connections can be difficult for a variety of reasons. It takes time and energy. Having appropriate social connections is a "have to have" not a "nice to have" issue to optimize psychological well-being. This is especially true during times of stress or transition. In terms of the whole lifespan, when we're young we have parents, school, sports, and other activities that regularly bring us into contact with other people. These regular meetings are an ideal context to form friendships, but as you move through life into adolescence and adulthood those opportunities become fewer and fewer. At the time when many men are having children, their opportunities to connect with people may diminish to work and home. The reality is that many men and dads have trouble being proactive about maintaining existing friendships and/or making new ones. Often without realizing it, dads gradually stop participating in their friendships and find themselves trying to get all of their support and connection needs met by just their partner. No matter how great your partner is, no one person can meet all of your social connection needs. The concept of a "social connection diet" is one in which everyone has his or her own unique set of interpersonal needs. It takes a variety of relationships—friends, family, romantic partner, kids, trusted colleagues—to meet these needs. The problem is that if you have only one real source of support, you're likely to:

- Feel isolated
- Risk burning out the one person who supports you
- At some level, resent that person for not being able to meet all of your needs

Most importantly, if something happens to your sole source of support, you fall hard!

You don't need many best friends, but you do need at least four supportive people other than a romantic partner or your family. If something happens to one or more of them, you will still have stability and support during tough times.

Changing How You Communicate

Meeting new people and putting in the effort to stay connected with them over time may be difficult. One relatively simple way to start the process is to think of people who you already know, and with whom you already communicate. Without having to even change what you communicate you can take an initial step to:

1. Increase the frequency of communication
2. Change the medium to make it more immediate
3. Talk about more direct/personal topics

If you only email with the person, start sending text messages. If you only text, occasionally pick up the phone. If your reaction is, "I hate the phone because I prefer to talk in person" or "It's awkward to speak on the phone" then you are most likely engaging in anxiety-driven avoidance. This might be holding you back from getting more out of your friendships. Simply by communicating more frequently and immediately, you can have better connections.

Men tend to get to know each through indirect communications. They don't talk about themselves, but rather about some external topic such as work, a game, sports, a project, a mutual acquaintance, or a TV show. They explore agreements or disagreements. Over time, the relationship can be measured by increased directness. They talk more directly about themselves, what's important to them, and even some areas of difficulty they're experiencing.

Is the Relationship a Good Fit?

Not all friendships are equal. The most straightforward way to determine if a relationship is working is by taking a concrete look at the fit for both people involved. This fit (friendships, romance, family, colleagues) is evidenced by the extent to which each person's needs are met. It's important to remember that *no one relationship can meet all of your needs,* therefore, you need to diversify your sources. If you have a clear sense of what your own needs are (e.g. the other person responds promptly when you contact her/him, keeps your secrets, helps out when you're in a tough patch), and some understanding of what the other person is looking for, you can best gauge if the relationship is a fit. Don't try to force it; you'll probably be able to feel it. Try to figure out where the disconnect is, accept the limitation on the relationship with that person, and then move on to connect with someone else who's a better match. There's no failing or succeeding in relationships—they either fit, or they don't.

Dads commonly use justifications like "pity party," "dirty laundry," "looking weak," "none of their business," "it won't help," "it's been too long, so it'll be awkward to reach out now," or "they won't get it" to avoid talking with supportive people in their lives. The reality is that you usually feel better after talking about what's bothering you—and it actually takes more strength to risk talking than it does to let anxiety drive avoidance and "stuff it."

One final important point to keep in mind is that the more you develop supportive relationships, the more chances you'll have to be there and support others when they hit inevitable difficult phases in life.

Putting Into Practice: Four Pillars of Self-Care

In this chapter, you learned about four pillars of self-care that are essential for all new parents to work on. The way that you get to do these parts of your life will probably look different in the first year postpartum than it did before the birth, but sleep, diet, exercise, and social support are still key for moms and dads. A great way to keep these from falling off the radar is for dads to focus on one pillar at a time and keep a basic log of how they engage in behaviors related to self-care. For example, for social support, he might have a note pad application in his phone and at the end of the week, note "video chat with my brother, coffee with a friend, breakfast with my partner." The following week, he would focus on a different pillar such as exercise or sleep. As noted in the Family Logistics Meeting section at the end of Chapter 5, couples communicating about how they are doing is essential for accountability and staying healthy.

Chapter 7

A CALL TO ACTION

We invite you to join the Parental Mental Health Movement. Social advocacy and action are required to meet the needs of ALL pregnant and postpartum families. Our children will benefit from listening to and supporting both parents.

1. Give acknowledgement: The fact is an egg requires a sperm for pregnancy. Nature takes over the woman's body, so naturally, she becomes the focus of attention. What about the "pregnant" man? Who listens to his joys and fears?

2. Pay attention: Anthropologists have observed in some cultures a male experience of pregnancy called "couvade." Some men exhibit somatic symptoms that are overlooked and misinterpreted. We need to pay attention to the medical needs of men too.

3. Ask thoughtful questions: The pregnant couple is transitioning from being a duo to parenthood. As individuals, and together, they are entering a new phase of life. This journey is scary as well as exciting. They are facing challenges, decisions, and fears. Pregnancy is a time to have conversations. Who will provide a safe environment where they can talk, cry, and get support without being judged?

4. Know the truth: Having a baby is hard on relationships and marriage. Statistics challenge the hope that the addition of a baby will preserve or even improve partnerships.

5. Men have hormones too: A series of studies have shown that men do experience hormonal shifts similar to women's around the birth of their babies, although the magnitude of the change is less for fathers than it is for mothers.

6. Watch for depression and anxiety: Statistically, rates of postpartum depression are similar in fathers and mothers, and rates of anxiety are high for all new parents. We know who is at risk. It is essential to be frank about personal and family histories of mental illness. There is no shame acknowledging the truth. Stigma does nothing but keep one from getting help.

7. Keys for wellness: Fathers and mothers need to sleep, eat well, exercise, have time for themselves, share their emotions and get support. Pregnancy and the postpartum period wreck routines. It is not easy to accept help, but it is a foundation for successful parenting and well-being.

8. Embrace gender-inclusive language: Everyone needs to be heard.

9. Recognize and question harmful and sexist assumptions about men and masculinities: When dads completely put aside their own needs, it reaffirms harmful stereotypes that tend to cause anxiety and depression. Take time to ask a dad, "How are you doing? How are you REALLY doing?" and then be willing to listen if he takes the risk to tell you.

10. Take action: Start this conversation within yourself and your community and make a difference.

ABOUT THE AUTHORS

Jane I. Honikman

I was born in 1945 in Palo Alto, California where my two older brothers and I attended the local schools. We lived a stable and middle-class lifestyle. Our father had his own business while our mother was a traditional homemaker and community volunteer. My ambition was to be just like my mother. I graduated from Whittier College in 1967 with a BA in Sociology, got married, and three years later, moved to Santa Barbara, California.

In the 1970s, we became parents. I began to feel the paralyzing guilt of not being able to cope and function in my new role. Frustrated by the lack of community support, I co-founded Postpartum Education for Parents (PEP) to ensure support for myself and other new parents. The organization has thrived in Santa Barbara because of trained parent volunteers.

I had unintentionally begun a career as a parent support advocate. In 1980, I was awarded a Project/Research grant from the American Association of University Women to conduct A Study of the Dynamics and Development of Postpartum Support Groups. It was designed to serve as a first step in the formation of a National Network of Postpartum Support Groups. In 1984, I was invited to present about PEP at an international scientific conference on postpartum psychiatric illness. Three years later, I founded

Postpartum Support International (PSI). It was headquartered in our home for the next eighteen years.

During the 1990s, I traveled to and gave presentations at national and global meetings promoting perinatal mental health and preventing mental illness. In 1995, I completed a master's degree in psychology and began teaching. After retiring as Executive Director of PSI, I co-founded the Postpartum Action Institute (PAI) to continue my long-term goal to confront the stigma of mental illness and the mythology surrounding new parenthood. I have authored books, articles, and educational materials on parental mental health. My own family includes my supportive husband, three adult children, their spouses, and eight grandchildren.

Daniel B. Singley

I was born the youngest of three brothers in 1973 in Houston, Texas. Our dad traveled frequently for work. We moved to Holland when I was one, and then to Switzerland when I was three, returning to Houston when I was six. After graduating from high school, I went to college at the University of Virginia where I studied pre-med basic sciences and majored in Spanish and Latin American literature.

After college, I spent 1996 traveling around Southeast Asia, living in Taiwan, and building a house for a schoolteacher in a tiny rural town in Costa Rica. I married in 2000 and began a PhD program in Counseling Psychology at the University of Maryland. I was involved in research as well as psychotherapy, training with a focus in the areas of White racial identity development, career counseling, and positive psychology.

Our first son was born in July 2004 and there was little information for me when my wife was pregnant. We moved to San Diego for my internship at the University of California, San Diego, and three weeks into it, a guest speaker (now my close friend and mentor, Dr. Jeff Jones) lectured on the psychology of men, masculinity, and focusing on new dads' mental health. No one had ever talked to me about these issues in psychology. I had a one-month-old at the time, so my identity as a man and a father were front and center for me. In psychology, we say that "research is me-search," and as soon as I finished my internship and post-doc, I began to focus my career on men's issues with an emphasis on early fatherhood.

In 2007, a year after my younger son was born, I was awarded a California First 5 grant to develop Basic Training for New Dads classes, and I also started conducting research on new dads' involvement with their babies. Not long after, I founded the Center for Men's Excellence as my professional home so I could concentrate my work on men's mental health issues including early fatherhood.

These days, it's a struggle, but my wife and I try to have a work/life balance. It's not an accident that I've become an expert in fatherhood, and my own development in my role as a father has been a real thrill. In fact, it's in large part due to my wife and boys' support and interest in the work I do that I've been able to (usually) balance working hard and parenting hard! Over the past decade or so, I've been very happy to be able to play a huge part in my wife and kids' lives while also having the opportunity to travel around the country conducting trainings, attending conferences, and serving on boards of truly inspired—and inspiring—organizations, including Postpartum Support International (which, of course, Jane founded), the San Diego Psychological Association, and the American Psychological Association's Society for the Psychological Study of Men and Masculinities. In my free time, I surf, cook, read, hang out with my wife and friends, and think up new ways for my boys and me to go out and explore the world together.

TOOLS THAT ROCK

Resources for Dads and the People Who Support Them

Padre Cadre: www.padrecadre.com

Life of Dad: www.lifeofdad.com

Basic Training for New Dads: www.menexcel.com

Postpartum Support International: www.postpartum.net — Especially the monthly telephone "Dads Chat" which is free, anonymous, and a rare chance to connect with other new and expectant dads

The Good Men Project: www.goodmenproject.com/category/families

Daddit: www.reddit.com/r/daddit

Dad Labs: www.dadlabs.com

National Fatherhood Initiative: www.fatherhood.org

Facebook Dad Groups

New and Expecting Father's (Tha Man Cave): www.facebook.com/groups/551740815029578

Pregnant Dads & New Fathers Support Group: www.facebook.com/groups/167780370522770

Fathers and First Time Dads Support Group: www.facebook.com/groups/623873131145394

International Fathers' Mental Health Day: www.facebook.com/dadsMHday

Brand New Father Support Group: www.facebook.com/groups/bnfsupport

Postpartum Dads: www.facebook.com/PostpartumDads

Expecting Father's Support Group: www.facebook.com/groups/1524473641126632

DaddiLife Force: www.facebook.com/groups/143366569493037

Glad to be Called Dad: www.facebook.com/groups/1524473641126632

REFERENCES

American Pregnancy Association, www.americanpregnancy.org

American Psychiatric Association. 2018. "Position Statement on Peer Support." https://www.psychiatry.org/File%20Library/About-APA/Organization-Documents-Policies/Policies/Position-2018-Peer-Support-Services.pdf.

Baker, K. 2019. "Priorities in Male Psychology." British Psychological Society. https://thepsychologist.bps.org.uk/volume-31/november-2018/priorities-male-psychology.

Bosson, J. K., & Vandello, J. A. 2011. "Precarious manhood and its links to action and aggression." *Current Directions in Psychological Science,* 20 (2), 82-86.

Brennan, A. 2014. "Couvade syndrome: why some men develop signs of pregnancy." *The Conversation, Health and Medicine.*

British Psychological Society. 2016. "Achieving representation in psychology." https://thepsychologist.bps.org.uk. Vol 29.

Burns, D. 1989. *The Feeling Good Handbook.* William Morrow and Company.

Carlson, D., Hanson, S., & Fitzroy, A. 2016. "The Division of Child Care, Sexual Intimacy, and Relationship Quality in Couples." *Psychology.*

Chuick, C. D., Greenfeld, J. M., et al. 2009. "A qualitative investigation of depression in men." American Psychological Association. PsycNET.apa.org

Clinton, J. 1986. "Expectant fathers at risk for couvade." *Nursing Research,* 35 (5), 290-295.

Cochran, S. V., & Rabinowitz, F. E. 1999. "Men and depression: Clinical and empirical perspectives." Elsevier.

Coffman, J., Bates, T., Geyn, I., & Spetz, J. 2018. "California's Current and Future Behavioral Health Workforce." Research Report, Healthforce Center, the University of California San Francisco.

Cotter, D., Hermsen, J. & Vanneman, R. 2004. "Gender inequality at work." *Psychology.*

David, D. S., & Brannon, R. (Eds.). 1976. "The forty-nine percent majority: The male sex role." Addison Wesley Publishing Company.

Davis, D., Logsdon, M. C., & Birkmer, J. 1996. "Types of support expected and received by mothers after their infants' discharge from the NICU." *Issues in Comprehensive Pediatric Nursing.* 19 (4), 263-73.

Dinkmeyer, D. & McKay, G. 1976. *Systematic Training for Effective Parenting.* West Virginia; STEP Publishers, LLC.

Eddy, B., Poll, V., Whiting, J., & Clevesy, M. 2019. "Forgotten Fathers: Postpartum Depression in Men." *Journal of Family Issues,* 40 (8), 1001-1017.

Erikson, E. H. 1950. "Growth and crises of the 'healthy personality.'"

Frisco, M. L., & Williams, K. 2003. "Perceived housework equity, marital happiness, and divorce in dual-earner households." *Journal of Family Issues,* 24, 51-73.

Gettler, T. G., McDade, T. W., Fernail, A. B., & Kuzawa, C. W. 2011. "Longitudinal evidence that fatherhood decreases testosterone in human males." Proceedings of the National Academy of Sciences of the United States of America. 108 (39), 16194-16199. Accessed November 17, 2019. https://www.pnas.org/content/108/39/16194

Gottman, J. M., & Silver, N. 2015. "The seven principles for making marriage work: A practical guide from the country's foremost relationship expert." Harmony.

Greenberg, S. T., Shepard, S. J., Cochran, S. V., & Haley, J. T. 2009. "A qualitative investigation of depression in men." *Psychology of Men & Masculinity,* 10 (4), 302.

Hauser, L. & Freeman, D. 2009. *The Legacy Family: The Definitive Guide to Creating a Successful Multigenerational Family.* New York: Palgrave Macmillan.

Hyde, J. S. 2005. "The gender similarities hypothesis." *American Psychologist,* 60 (6), 581.

Kiselica, M. S., & Englar-Carlson, M. 2010. "Identifying, affirming, and building upon male strengths: The positive psychology/positive masculinity model of psychotherapy with boys and men." *Psychotherapy: Theory, Research, Practice, Training,* 47 (3), 276.

Kornich, S., Brines, J., & Leupp, K. 2013. "Egalitarianism, Housework and Sexual Frequency in Marriage." *American Sociological Review.* 78 (1), 26-50.

Kuo, P. X., Braungart-Rieker, J. M., Lefever, J. E. B., Sarma, M. S., O'Neill, M., & Gettler, L. T. 2018. "Fathers' cortisol and testosterone in the days around infants' births predict later paternal involvement." *Hormones and Behavior,* 106, 28-34.

Lipkin, M. & Lamb, G. S. 1982. "The couvade syndrome: an epidemiologic study." *Annals of Internal Medicine,* 96 (509-511).

O'Neil, J. M. 2008. "Summarizing 25 years of research on men's gender role conflict using the Gender Role Conflict Scale: New research paradigms and clinical implications." *The Counseling Psychologist,* 36 (3), 358-445.

"Americans Widely Support Paid Family and Medical Leave, but Differ Over Specific Policies." Pew Research Center, Washington, D.C. (March 23, 2017)* https://www.pewsocialtrends.org/2017/03/23/americans-widely-support-paid-family-and-medical-leave-but-differ-over-specific-policies/

"Modern Parenthood: Roles of Moms and Dads Converge as They Balance Work and Family." Pew Research Center, Washington, D.C. (March 14, 2013)* https://www.pewsocialtrends.org/2013/03/14/modern-parenthood-roles-of-moms-and-dads-converge-as-they-balance-work-and-family/

"Raising Kids and Running a Household: How Working Parents Share the Load." Pew Research Center, Washington, D.C. (November 4, 2015)* https://www.pewsocialtrends.org/2015/11/04/raising-kids-and-running-a-household-how-working-parents-share-the-load/

Pleck, J. H. 1981. "Three Conceptual Issues in Research on Male Roles (No. 98)." Wellesley College, Center for Research on Women.

Pollack, W. 1998. "Real Boys." Random House Audio Publishing.

Rabinowitz, F. E., & Cochran, S. V. 2008. "Men and therapy: A case of masked male depression." *Clinical Case Studies,* 7 (6), 575-591.

Rosenberg, J., & Wilcox, W. B. 2006. "The importance of fathers in the healthy development of children." US Department Health and Human Services, Administration for Children and Families, Administration on Children, Youth and Families, Children's Bureau, Office of Child Abuse and Neglect.

Saxbe, D. E., Schetter, C. D., Simon, C. D., Adam, E. K., & Shalowitz, M. U. 2017. "High paternal testosterone may protect against postpartum depressive symptoms in fathers, but confer risk to mothers and children." *Hormones and Behavior,* 95, 103-112.

Silverstein, L. B., & Auerbach, C. F. 1999. "Deconstructing the essential father." *American Psychologist,* 54 (6), 397.

Silverstein, L. B., Auerbach, C. F., & Levant, R. F. 2002. "Contemporary fathers reconstructing masculinity: Clinical implications of gender role strain." *Professional Psychology: Research and Practice,* 33 (4), 361.

Singley, D. B., & Edwards, L. 2015. "Men's perinatal mental health in the transition to fatherhood." *Professional Psychology Research and Practice,* 46 (5), 309-316.

Singley, D. B., Cole, B. P., Hammer, J. H., Molloy, S., Rowell, A., & Isacco, A. 2018. "Development and psychometric evaluation of the Paternal Involvement With Infants Scale." *Psychology of Men & Masculinity,* 19 (2), 167.

Smuts, B. B., & Gubernick, D. J. 1992. "Male-infant relationships in nonhuman primates: Paternal investment or mating effort." *Father-Child relations: Cultural and Biosocial Contexts,* 1-30.

Storey, A. E., et al. 2000. "Hormonal correlates of paternal responsiveness in new and expectant fathers." *Evolution & Human Behavior,* 21, 79-95

Trivers, R. L. 1972. "Parental investments and sexual selection." *Reproductive Strategies,* 52-95. Reprinted from *Sexual Selection and the Descent of Man.* Chicago: Aldine Publishing, 136-179.

United Kingdom Mental Health Foundation. 2016. "Survey of people with lived experience of mental health problems reveals men less likely to seek medical support." Accessed November 24, 2019. https://www.mentalhealth.org.uk/news/survey-people-lived-experience-mental-health-problems-reveals-men-less-likely-seek-medical

Vogel, D. L., & Heath, P. J. 2016. "Men, masculinities, and help-seeking patterns." In Wong, Y. Joel (Ed.) & Wester, Stephen R. (Ed.). 2016. "APA handbook of men and masculinities." Washington, DC: American Psychological Association, 685-707.

Wisner, K. L., Sit, D. K., McShea, M. C., Rizzo, D. M., Zoretich, R. A., Hughes, C. L., Eng H. F., Luther, J. F., Wisniewski, S. R., Costantino, M. L., Confer, A. L., Moses-Kolko, E. L., Famy, C. S., & Hanusa, B. H. 2013. "Onset timing, thoughts of self-harm, and diagnoses in postpartum women with screen-positive depression findings." *JAMA Psychiatry,* 70 (5), 490-498.

World Health Organization. 2004. "Prevention of Mental Disorders. Effective interventions and policy options." Summary Report. Part I, page 21.

**Pew Research Center bears no responsibility for the analyses or interpretations of the data presented here. The opinions expressed herein, including any implications for policy, are those of the author and not of Pew Research Center.*